Jesus Is My Very Best Friend

Jesus Is My Very Best Friend

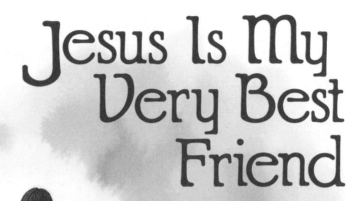

written by
Barbara A. Young

illustrated by
Kathy Mitter

CONCORDIA®
Publishing House
St. Louis

Jesus is my very best Friend.

He takes good care of me
and gives me everything I need.

Jesus gives me strength to play

and a warm bed to sleep in.

He gives me
all the good things I eat and drink.

His love makes me happy every day.

Jesus is always near me,
and He shows me how to live.

When I am afraid, I know He is near.

When bad things happen to me,
I talk to Jesus about them.

I know He hears and listens to me.

When others are unkind to me,
I know He still loves me.

When I am sick or get hurt,
I know He will be with me.

I am glad to know Jesus loves me
and will be with me always.

I will love Him and
follow Him all of my life.

Jesus is

my very best Friend.